THE ICE CREAM DREAM

Written by: **Patricia Fine**
Illustrated by: **John Portez**

An Original Playbook®
presented in....
Playbook® Advantage Format

© 2004 PLAYBOOKS, INC. LAGUNA HILLS, CALIFORNIA, ALL RIGHTS RESERVED.

RS 1-4
GLC 1-5
Story Length: 2,587 Words

The Ice Cream Dream

PUBLISHED BY PLAYBOOKS, INC.
d.b.a. Playbooks Reader's Theater

Copyright © 2004 by Playbooks, Inc., Lake Forest, CA.
All Rights Reserved.

Playbook, Playbooks, Playbook Format, Roleplay Reader,
Playberized, StageBooks, and Being a Start Makes Reading Fun
are trademarks of Playbook, Inc.

ISBN 978-1-60476-018-7

The unique format of a Playbook® with character colorization and specialized readability levels is a proprietary method of book structure, writing, format, construction, re-construction, displaying and printing protected under U.S. Patent Nos. 6,683,611, 6,859,206, and 7,456,834 with additional patents pending. For information regarding licensing the rights to write, edit, construct, re-construct, display, print or publish any book in Playbook® format call 1-800-375-2926. No part of this publication may be reproduced in whole or in part, or stored in a retrieval system, or transmitted in any form or by any means, electronic, mechanical, photocopying, recording, or otherwise, without written permission of the publisher, except by a reviewer, who may quote brief passages in a review. For information regarding permission, call Playbooks, Inc. at 1-800-375-2926. This book is subject to the condition that it shall not, by way of trade or otherwise, be re-sold, hired out, or otherwise circulated without the publisher's prior consent in any form of binding or cover other than that in which it is published and without a similar condition including this condition being imposed on the subsequent purchaser. Performances of this story/script may be videotaped for school or library purposes.

Being a Star Makes Reading Fun™

Welcome to the world of Playbooks® and the beginning of a wonderful role-play reading adventure! Playbook® stories are presented in a unique and colorful format and are read out loud by several readers like a play, without memorization, props, or a stage. When you read a Playbook®, you and other readers bring the story to life and become the characters. As you read **your** part out loud, you will have fun expressing and acting like your character. You and the other readers will explore the story plot together and learn what will happen next. It's an exciting journey of discovery that pulls you into the story, and you'll want to read it out loud again and again!

HOW TO GET STARTED

Begin your reading adventure with the **Character Summary** here at the beginning of the book. **You'll notice right away that the words and sentences for each character appear in a different color here and throughout the book. This will make it easy to follow along and read your part with confidence and enthusiasm.**

It doesn't matter whether you are a beginning reader or an experienced reader; there is a part for everyone. The number of characters in the story may not match the number of readers in your group and that's okay. Readers can play more than one character role, or readers can share a role by taking turns.

Once your role has been assigned, you and the other readers will each read his or her character's summary out loud from his or her own copy of the book. The most experienced reader typically reads the narrator's role.
It's important for teachers and parents to refer to the Teacher or Parent Guide when assigning roles.

Have fun bringing your character to life by bringing your voice up and down, speaking softly or loudly, changing your facial expressions, and moving your hands or body. Trying different voices or accents can also be lots of fun.

Sometimes you will see *black italicized text* inside parenthesis before or in the middle of sentences. **These are called "cues" and tell you how to read a sentence with expression.** For example, if the "cue" says *(with surprise),* speak the sentence with surprise in your voice! Cues are not read out loud.

MAKING THE MOST OF THE STORY

It's more fun to read the story out loud together with other readers the first time you read your role. It's exciting to discover the story in this way rather than each reader practicing his or her part alone first. As you get better with your role, you may want to change the way you express your character's personality, or you may want to switch roles with another reader. Be creative! When all your readers get comfortable with their roles, you may want to read the story in front of a friendly audience.

Reading out loud is so much fun that it's easy to forget about the other readers. **So be sure to read with good manners!** Here are some helpful hints. Stay quiet when other readers are reading. Follow along and keep up and be ready to read when it's your turn. Speak loudly and clearly so everyone can hear you. Stay in character for the whole story! Most importantly, enjoy your role-play reading experience. **You and your cast of characters are ready to begin your Playbook® adventure!**

FOR TEACHERS AND PARENTS

For specific guidance on implementing a Playbook® story in the classroom or in the home, download a FREE Teacher or Parent Guide at the following link.
http://www.readerstheater.com/teacherguide.pdf

It's important for students to be assigned a role they can read with success in front of their peers. A "Recommended Reader Assignment" chart that identifies the reading level for each story character is included in this story's group set. To print additional copies, visit www.readerstheater.com/rra.html and locate the story's title.

Being an active participant in a story spikes the reader's curiosity to learn more about the story's theme. Rewarding a child for exceptional effort and performance is an excellent practice for boosting a child's reading confidence. To download **FREE Award Certificates** to recognize star performers, visit www.readerstheater.com/awardcertificates.pdf.

Playbooks, Inc. also provides story-specific activity suggestions and worksheets to reinforce concepts and go beyond the story into the content areas of Language Arts, Math, Science, Social Studies, Art, Health, etc., as well as Character Development. Activities range in skill level and age-appropriateness, so the teacher or parent can choose activities that best suit the readers. Activities include comprehension quizzes, crossword puzzles, word search, vocabulary, discussion and writing prompts, story mapping, word problems, etc. To download FREE supplemental activity sheets for this and other stories, visit
www.readerstheater.com/supplements.html.

Seeing children develop a passion for reading while working with the Playbook® format will be one of your greatest rewards.

Character Summary

Before beginning this story, it is helpful for each reader to read his/her character's summary aloud.

Mr. MacRicee

I love ice cream. I eat it every day. It is sooo good. I like chocolate best.

Store Clerk

I am a clerk. Sometimes I work at the Sweet Treat Shop, and sometimes I work at the food store. Sometimes I even work at the store where they sell things like TV sets and freezers. I sell Mr. MacRicee all he needs.

Vanilla Ice Cream

I am creamy vanilla, but I can change into other flavors, too. I talk to Mr. MacRicee all the time, and he listens to me. I always have good ideas to share!

Character Summary

Before beginning this story, it is helpful for each reader to read his/her character's summary aloud.

Chocolate Ice Cream

I am yummy chocolate, but I can also change into other flavors ... many more than my dear friend, Vanilla. When I talk, Mr. MacRicee always listens. It's not that I'm bossy, I just have better ideas than other flavors.

Strawberry Ice Cream

I am fruity strawberry, and I can change into any flavor you can name with no problem at all. I'm sure that Mr. MacRicee likes me best. I know that my ideas are much better than the other flavors.

Narrator

As the narrator, I am the master storyteller! It's up to me to keep the story interesting with each exciting detail.

What is Cue Text? Cue text tells readers HOW to read their lines. Cue text is shown in both italics and parentheses and appears before a line of dialogue. **Cue text is not read aloud.**
Example: *(yelling)* Look out!

Chapter 1
Single-scoop

Narrator Once there was a man named Mr. MacRicee who liked ice cream. He didn't just like ice cream—he loved it! Whether it was in bars or cups or sandwiches or on a stick or in sundaes, malts, sodas, or floats, he loved it all. It was as if ice cream spoke to him. Every night after dinner, he would walk down to the Sweet Treat Ice Cream Shop for a single scoop cone.

Store Clerk	Well, hello there, Mr. MacRicee. What kind of ice cream cone will it be this time?
Mr. MacRicee	Let me see. This is so hard.
Vanilla	Choose me! I'm Vanilla. I'm creamy and smooth.
Chocolate	No! Choose me! I'm Chocolate. I'm sweet and yummy.
Strawberry	No! No! Choose me! I'm Strawberry. I taste like ripe fruit.
Store Clerk	So what do you think? What kind do you feel like tonight?
Mr. MacRicee	Oh! I will have Chocolate, Vanilla, and Strawberry.
All Cones	Great Choice, Mr. MacRicee!

Store Clerk	Three scoops, eh? Very good!
Narrator	Mr. MacRicee soon decided that three scoops were always better than just one, so from then on, he started to order triples. The day soon came, though, when other flavors were getting his attention.
Store Clerk	What would you like to try today, Mr. MacRicee?
Vanilla	Choose me! I'm Rocky Road. I'm filled with walnuts and marshmallows.
Chocolate	No! Choose me! I'm Butter Pecan. I have a rich, nutty taste.
Strawberry	No! No! Choose me! I'm English Toffee. My bite-sized candy pieces are so good!

Mr. MacRicee	Hmm … let me see. Maybe I will have all of those, too!
All Cones	Good thinking, Mr. MacRicee!
Store Clerk	Do you mean a triple cone with Butter Pecan, Rocky Road, and English Toffee?
Mr. MacRicee	Yes, for one of my cones … and my other....
Store Clerk	So then you want another cone with Vanilla, Chocolate, and Strawberry?
Mr. MacRicee	Yes, please. That is what I said.
Store Clerk	Yes, sir, Mr. MacRicee. All very good choices!
Narrator	One day, Mr. MacRicee was sitting in his living room, thinking about his favorite subject. You guessed it, ice cream!
Mr. MacRicee	I love ice cream after dinner.
Vanilla	But you also like it after lunch. That is true, isn't it?
Chocolate	And you also like it after breakfast. That is true, isn't it?
Strawberry	And you also like it as a snack. That is true, isn't it?
Mr. MacRicee	Yes, that is all true. I like it all day.

Vanilla	So, why don't you have a triple-scoop cone after lunch?
Chocolate	And two triple-scoop cones after dinner?
Strawberry	And a triple-scoop cone after breakfast to start your day?
Mr. MacRicee	I do not think the Sweet Treat Shop is open for breakfast.
Vanilla	That's not a problem.
Chocolate	No problem at all.
Strawberry	There's no problem here!
Mr. MacRicee	What do you mean?
Vanilla	Well, you have a refrigerator, don't you?
Chocolate	Well, it has a freezer section, doesn't it?
Strawberry	Well, it's full of ice cream, isn't it?
Mr. MacRicee	No, it is not.
Vanilla	But it could be….
Chocolate	And it would be….
Strawberry	And it should be….
Mr. MacRicee	What do you mean?
Vanilla	You could go to the grocery store.
Chocolate	That would be a good idea.
Strawberry	And you should buy ice cream in cartons!

Mr. MacRicee	What kind?
Vanilla	Oh, let's see ... a pint of Coconut Pineapple.
Chocolate	Oh, let's see ... a pint of Wild Raspberry.
Strawberry	Oh, let's see ... a pint of Black Cherry!
Mr. MacRicee	That does it! I am going to the store!

Chapter 2
Double Dipping

Narrator	In no time at all, Mr. MacRicee was wheeling a shopping cart through the store to the ice cream section.
Mr. MacRicee	Now, let me see….
Store Clerk	Can I help you, sir?
Mr. MacRicee	Yes, thank you. I need pints of ice cream.
Store Clerk	Right over here, sir, on your left.
Mr. MacRicee	Oh, they are small.
Vanilla	You're right! We should have said quarts.
Chocolate	You're right! We should have said gallons.
Strawberry	You're right! We should have said drums!
Mr. MacRicee	Now, now. Not so fast. This is very hard.

Vanilla	May I suggest some Butterscotch Ripple?
Chocolate	May I suggest some Chocolate Swirl?
Strawberry	May I suggest some Peppermint Twist?
Narrator	Mr. MacRicee quickly filled his shopping cart with six quarts of ice cream—the new flavors that had been suggested, and then his old favorites, Vanilla, Chocolate, and Strawberry.
Store Clerk	Are you ready, sir?
Mr. MacRicee	Yes, I am. Thank you for your help.
Store Clerk	Are you going to have a party with all that ice cream?
Mr. MacRicee	No, it is all for me.
Store Clerk	Oh, my!

Narrator	When he arrived home, he could hardly fit all the cartons into the freezer section of his refrigerator.
Vanilla	You don't need those vegetables. Get rid of them!
Chocolate	You don't need that meat. Get rid of it!
Strawberry	You don't need those frozen dinners. Get rid of them!
Mr. MacRicee	You are right. I will get rid of them. Then I can fit in more ice cream.
All cones	You are very smart, Mr. MacRicee!
Narrator	The next day, he returned to the store. He took a long time to choose.
Vanilla	How about some Chocolate Chip Cookie Dough?

Chocolate	How about some Peanut Crunch?
Strawberry	How about some Malted Milk Ball Crisp?
Narrator	When he came to the check out counter with his cart full of ice cream, the clerk was very surprised.
Store Clerk	Did you already eat all the ice cream you bought yesterday?
Mr. MacRicee	Well, I did eat a lot. But today, I need more.
Store Clerk	I guess you really like ice cream!
Narrator	At home, Mr. MacRicee had a hard job fitting all the cartons into the freezer section—even though he had gotten rid of all the other food.
Mr. MacRicee	There is no more room. I will have to eat a lot more ice cream today.
Chocolate	I have an idea! Tomorrow you need to go shopping.
Vanilla	I have an idea! Tomorrow you need to go to the appliance store.
Strawberry	I have an idea! Tomorrow you need to buy a freezer!
Mr. MacRicee	What a good idea! I am happy I had this idea. How big do you think…?

Vanilla	Three by five. Right?
Chocolate	Four by six. Right?
Strawberry	Five by seven. Right?
Mr. MacRicee	Right! A big one will be good.
Narrator	Mr. MacRicee bought a freezer the next day, and the day after that, it was brought to his house. He went to the store again to fill the new freezer with even more flavors of ice cream.
Store Clerk	My goodness! It's Mr. MacRicee again! Good morning, sir. More cartons of ice cream today?
Mr. MacRicee	Those cartons are too small. Do you have bigger ones?
Store Clerk	The half gallon size is very good for families, sir.
Vanilla	Half gallons are good. Especially if it's Pistachio Puff.
Chocolate	Half gallons are good. Especially if it's Black walnut Whip.
Strawberry	Half gallons are good. Especially if it's Pecan Crunch!

Narrator	The clerk told Mr. MacRicee to be careful when he lifted the heavy cartons down from the top shelf, but he was in a hurry, and he didn't listen. One of the cartons fell on his head, but he was so busy thinking about buying the ice cream that he didn't pay much attention to it.
Mr. MacRicee	Ouch!
Store Clerk	Are you hurt? Can I help you?
Mr. MacRicee	No, it is O.K. I will take all of those.
Store Clerk	All of the flavors in that case, sir?
Mr. MacRicee	Yes. That is what I said.
Store Clerk	Very well. I will help pack them for you.

Narrator	The grocery clerk could not believe his ears. But he packed all the half gallon flavors into several boxes and put them into Mr. MacRicee's car. He was a very good customer, and the clerk didn't want to make him angry.

Narrator	When Mr. MacRicee got home, he spent a lot of time putting all the new half gallons of ice cream away in his new freezer. Now he had plenty of space.
Vanilla	Tomorrow, how about some Chocolate Fudge?
Mr. MacRicee	Yes. That sounds good.
Chocolate	Tomorrow, how about some Chocolate Brownie?
Mr. MacRicee	That sounds even better.

Strawberry	Tomorrow, how about some Chocolate Chip?
Mr. MacRicee	Yes! Chocolate Chip!
Narrator	When tomorrow came, and Mr. MacRicee went shopping again, he found that he did not have much room left in his new freezer.
Mr. MacRicee	Now what can I do?
Vanilla	Buy another freezer.
Chocolate	Buy two more freezers.
Strawberry	Buy three more freezers!
Mr. MacRicee	I can do that, but where will I put them?
Vanilla	In the dining room … you will dine on … ice cream.
Chocolate	In the living room … you will live for … ice cream.
Strawberry	In the bedroom … you will wake up to … ice cream!
Mr. MacRicee	But what about my things?
Vanilla	Do you really need that couch?
Chocolate	Do you really need that dining room set?
Strawberry	Do you really need that bed?
Mr. MacRicee	Well, I….

Vanilla	What's the problem? You can sit on a freezer and watch TV.
Chocolate	What's the problem? You can eat on a freezer.
Strawberry	What's the problem? You can sleep on a freezer.
Narrator	Mr. MacRicee returned to the appliance store to buy more freezers.
Store Clerk	Good afternoon, sir. What can I show you today?
Mr. MacRicee	I want to see….
Store Clerk	Just a minute. Weren't you here yesterday? You bought a large freezer, right?

Mr. MacRicee	Yes, yes, I did.
Store Clerk	Is there a problem?
Mr. MacRicee	Oh, no. But I need more.
Store Clerk	How many more?
Vanilla	Three would be good.
Chocolate	Six would be better.
Strawberry	Nine would be best.
Mr. MacRicee	I will take nine more.
Store Clerk	Did you say nine?
Mr. MacRicee	Yes, I need nine more. When can you send them?
Store Clerk	To your store, sir?
Mr. MacRicee	No, to my house.
Store Clerk	Your house? May I ask you why you need nine, sir?
Mr. MacRicee	For my ice cream!
Store Clerk	Oh! Of course!

Chapter 3

Triple Threat

Narrator	Mr. MacRicee continued to eat ice cream day after day, meal after meal. In fact, it was the only thing he was eating. He soon noticed that his clothes were getting smaller.
Mr. MacRicee	Oh, my! These pants are too small. I need new ones.
Strawberry	Get size twenty!
Chocolate	Get size forty!
Vanilla	Get size sixty!
Narrator	A week later, at the grocery store, the clerk did not recognize Mr. MacRicee because he was so much fatter.
Store Clerk	Mr. MacRicee, is that you?
Mr. MacRicee	Yes it is!
Store Clerk	Oh, I'm sorry. You look different.
Mr. MacRicee	What do you mean?
Store Clerk	Well ... bigger? I like your shirt.
Mr. MacRicee	It is new. All my shirts are new.

Vanilla	And his sweaters. His old sweaters shrank.
Chocolate	And his coats. None of them fit any more.
Strawberry	Even his shoes. Even his feet got fatter!
Narrator	Mr. MacRicee continued to put on weight until he started to look rather like a giant tub of ice cream himself. He decided that it was too much trouble to go to the grocery store.

Narrator	So, he started to phone in his order and have it brought to his house.
Vanilla	A gallon of Cherry Cheesecake, I think….
Chocolate	And two gallons of Cookies and Cream, I think….
Strawberry	And three gallons of Rainbow Blast, I think….

Narrator Some weeks passed, and Mr. MacRicee found that he was so fat that he couldn't get through the doors of his house anymore.

Vanilla The doors are too narrow. Make them one foot wider.

Chocolate Too narrow! Make the doors two feet wider.

Strawberry Much too narrow! Make the doors three feet wider!

Narrator So, he had to call a carpenter to make the changes that were needed. After the carpenter made all the changes, Mr. MacRicee's house looked rather strange.

All Cones	You fixed the problem, Mr. MacRicee!
Mr. MacRicee	That is much better!
Narrator	At least now he could move from room to room, and, what was more important, he could get to the front door when the truck came with his daily supply of ice cream.
Vanilla	Ooh! Blackberry Delight with sugar cone bits!
Chocolate	Ooh! Cherry Swirl with chocolate-covered peanuts!
Strawberry	Ooh! Strawberry Cheesecake with almond pieces!
Mr. MacRicee	Right in here!
Store Clerk	Yes, sir, Mr. MacRicee.
Chocolate	Put some in the ten freezers in the bedroom.
Vanilla	Put some in the fifteen freezers in the living room.
Strawberry	Put some in the twenty freezers in the family room.
Store Clerk	How about the garage? Are there freezers there, too?

Mr. MacRicee	Well, only twenty-five.
Store Clerk	Twenty-five? Is that why your car is in the driveway?
Mr. MacRicee	Yes. There is no more room for it.
Store Clerk	I see. O.K. I will fill those freezers with ice cream, too.
Narrator	The man from the grocery store brought the whole truckload into the garage.

Chapter 4
Four Score

Narrator	The next day, at three in the morning, a terrible thing happened. The electricity went out on Mr. MacRicee's street. Because it was while he was sleeping, he didn't notice it at first, but when he got up and got ready for breakfast, he had a nasty surprise.
Vanilla	The ice cream is soft!
Chocolate	It's not just soft. It's runny!
Strawberry	It's not just runny. It's melting!
Mr. MacRicee	Melting! Why?

Narrator	**He soon found out that the electricity was off, and that the ice cream in all of his seventy freezers was melting. As the day got warmer, the ice cream started to melt faster.**
Vanilla	It's all over the floor!
Chocolate	**It's all over the rug!**
Strawberry	It's all over the carpet!
Narrator	**Soon, Mr. MacRicee was standing in a pool of melted ice cream.**
Mr. MacRicee	Oh, dear! Oh, dear! What shall I do?
Vanilla	It's running down the stairs!
Chocolate	**It's running out the door!**
Strawberry	It's running down the street!

Narrator	There was a terrible mess all over the place. And because the doors had been made wider, what little furniture he had left, and all the freezers, floated out of the house, too. They were all swirling around in the street in the melted ice cream.
Mr. MacRicee	Oh, goodness!
Vanilla	There are rivers of ice cream!
Chocolate	No, there are seas of ice cream!
Strawberry	No, no, there are oceans of ice cream!
Narrator	People who lived on Mr. MacRicee's street were screaming and shouting and running up on their porches and climbing trees to get away from the ice cream. Children were yelling and splashing in it like they would in rain puddles.

Narrator	Dogs were howling, and cats were yowling. There was noise and disorder everywhere. And then, the worst thing happened, Mr. MacRicee fell down and was swept away in the melted ice cream.
Mr. MacRicee	Help! Help! Save me!
All Cones	We will save you!
Vanilla	Wait. Can you swim?
Chocolate	No. Can you swim?
Strawberry	Of course not! Can you swim?
Store Clerk	Do not worry, Mr. MacRicee! I will save you!
Narrator	It was the man from the grocery store. He was rowing a small boat toward Mr. MacRicee through all the melted ice cream. But Mr. MacRicee was so fat that as soon as he climbed into the boat, it tipped over. When he came up for air, he hit his head on the boat.
Mr. MacRicee	Ouch!
Narrator	The last thing he remembered hearing was the grocery clerk saying….
Store Clerk	Are you hurt? Can I help you?

Narrator	**Suddenly he was back in the grocery store, in the ice cream section, with a cart full of half gallons of all different flavors. He felt a big bump on his head. He looked at himself carefully, and he was his normal size.**
Vanilla	Wow!
Narrator	**He rushed home without buying anything. He was thrilled to see the doors of his house were their normal size, too. There was no melted lake of ice cream, and his neighbors were acting quite normal, for them anyway.**
Chocolate	Whew!
Narrator	**He ran in and out of all the rooms, and only found one freezer.**
Strawberry	Whee!
Vanilla	So what happened?
Chocolate	It was all a dream!
Strawberry	More like a nightmare!
Mr. MacRicee	Yes, it was all an Ice Cream Dream!
Narrator	**So Mr. MacRicee had been hit on the head by a falling half-gallon of Chocolate Chip ice cream and had passed out.**

Narrator	All the rest of what happened was just a dream. He had dreamt the whole thing while he was lying in the ice cream section of the grocery store, in the middle of cartons of Vanilla, Chocolate, and Strawberry and many other flavors.
Mr. MacRicee	Oooh! My head!
Vanilla	Can you believe this?
Chocolate	You mean we're not real?
Strawberry	Of course, we're not real!
Narrator	Mr. MacRicee had learned his lesson. Did he still like ice cream? Of course! But he was never greedy with it again. He took all the ice cream that was stored in his freezer and gave a party for the children in his neighborhood.

Narrator	Then he gave the large freezer to a local club that helped needy families. The freezer section of his regular refrigerator had plenty of room for the small amount of ice cream he now kept in it.
	Mr. MacRicee still walks down to the Sweet Treat Shop for a cone every once in a while, but now he only gets a single-scoop. He had learned his lesson about indulging and overeating unhealthy foods. Also, he now gets frozen yogurt instead of ice cream because it's healthier and tastes just as sweet.
Vanilla	Is this story over now?
Chocolate	I hope so. We already have parts in another story.
Mr. MacRicee	Thank goodness!
Strawberry	Let's go then, or we'll be late!

The End

A Word About Anagrams

If you look at the name, "MacRicee," you will see that if you change the letters around they spell "ice cream." When you change letters around like this, you have made an anagram.

You can try it with short words with only three letters, for example, "top" can be changed to "pot" or even "opt."

You can try it with your own name, for example, my name "Pat" can be changed to "tap" or "apt."

You can use longer words with four or five letters, for example, "tale" can be changed to "late," and "adobe" can be changed to "abode."

I am sure that you will be able to think of all kinds of great anagrams. Why not give it a try using your own name!

MEASUREMENTS TO LEARN

Dry and Liquid Measurements

1 scoop of ice cream	=	4 ounces (oz.)
4 ounces	=	1/4 pint (pt.), or 1/2 cup (c.)
8 ounces	=	1/2 pint, or 1 cup
2 pints	=	1 quart (qt.), or 4 cups
4 quarts	=	1 gallon (gal.), or 16 cups
1 drum	=	5 gallons
16 ounces	=	1 pound (lb.)
2,000 pounds	=	1 ton (t.)

www.ingramcontent.com/pod-product-compliance
Lightning Source LLC
Chambersburg PA
CBHW061806070526
44586CB00023B/2733